DRAW KAWA...
CUTE
PEOPLE
step-by-step

By Isobel
Lundie

BOOK HOUSE
a SALARIYA imprint

Author and illustrator:

Isobel Lundie graduated from Kingston University in 2015 where she studied illustration and animation. She is interested in how colourful and distinctive artwork can transform stories for children.

Published in Great Britain in MMXX by Book House, an imprint of The Salariya Book Company Ltd 25 Marlborough Place, Brighton BN1 1UB www.salariya.com

PB ISBN: 978-1-912904-42-6

SCRIBO   BOOK HOUSE   SCRIBBLERS

1 3 5 7 9 8 6 4 2

A CIP catalogue record for this book is available from the British Library.

Printed and bound in China.

Visit
www.salariya.com
for our online catalogue and **free** fun stuff.

PAPER FROM
SUSTAINABLE
FORESTS

DRAW KAWAII
CUTE
PEOPLE
step-by-step

By Isobel Lundie

contents

Introduction
what is kawaii?

Kawaii means 'cute' in the Japanese language but a Japanese art style has evolved which is also known as 'kawaii'. This style emphasises the 'cuteness' of the characters it depicts.

This book shows you how to master the techniques required to draw your own 'kawaii' people pictures. It includes tips and general information before you start and then a series of step-by-step projects for you to follow.

Materials

Pencil
Drawing with an HB pencil makes it easy to erase any unwanted excess lines.

Materials
The ideas in this book can be done in different ways and with different materials. Here are some suggestions.

coloured paper
Try drawing kawaii people on coloured paper!

coloured pencils
Coloured pencils are ideal for shading. See this ninja warrior drawing.

Labels

Make your own kawaii labels for your presents.

Ink

Use a small brush to make cute inky paintings!

Stickers

Draw onto stickers to make cute drawings for your friends!

Sketchbook

Use a sketchbook so you can keep all your drawings together.

Making everything cute

soften shapes

Rounding off the points of a triangle softens its shape. Try softening the edges of shapes when drawing your kawaii characters.

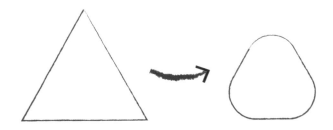

Simplify drawings

Make your drawing cuter by simplifying it down to its key features. This way you can make almost anything cute!

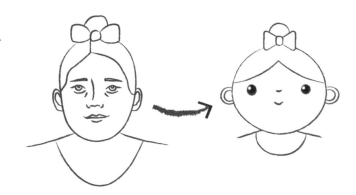

Proportions

The kawaii body should be proportioned as shown. A large head, with a short body and short legs.

Add a cute face

You can make almost anything cute by drawing an appealing cartoon face on it.

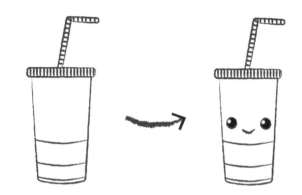

colours to soften

Pastel colours are cuter. Try using soft pastel colours to make your characters cuter.

Motion lines

Adding motion lines in this way is a simple and effective way to convey movement in a drawing.

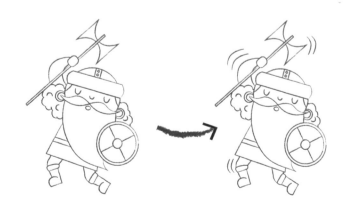

Adding accessories

cute shoes
Don't forget to add a pair of adorably cute shoes!

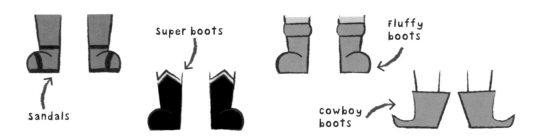

Super boots

Fluffy boots

Sandals

cowboy boots

cute stuff
Choose interesting objects to help bring your characters to life!

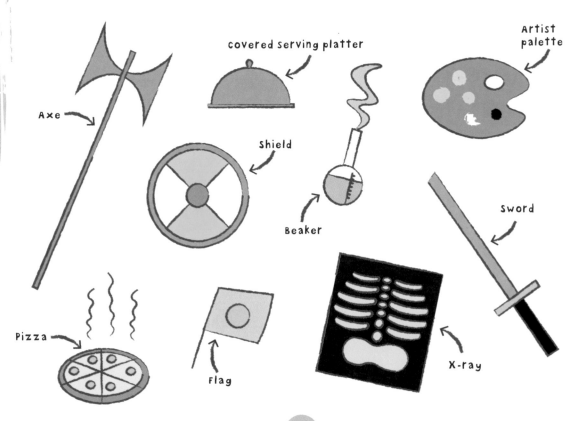

Artist palette

covered serving platter

Axe

Shield

Beaker

Sword

Pizza

Flag

X-ray

cute glasses

Huge glasses on a big head can be very cute.

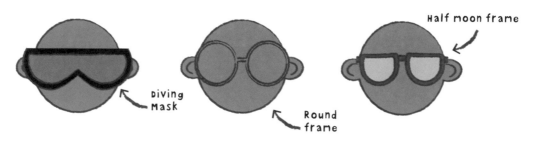

Half moon frame

Diving Mask

Round frame

cute hats

Adding a hat is an easy way to give your kawaii character style or identity!

chef's hat

Police hat

Egyptian headdress

Explorer hat

cowboy hat

Pilot hat

Beret

Hard hat

Sailor hat

Headdress

Expressions

change your character's expression to add personality.

Happy

Draw scrunched-up eyes.

Sad

Draw curved eyebrows.

Angry

Draw downturned eyebrows.

confused

Draw one eyebrow raised.

Scared

Both eyebrows raised.

Excited

Make the mouth wider.

crying

Draw in flowing tears.

Tired

Close the eyes.

Embarrassed

Purse the mouth.

Hairstyles

Experiment with different looks.

Long and wavy

Short bob

Bun head

crop cut

Wavy

Tight curls

Flicky bob

Bald and beardy

Bunches

Kawaii builder

1

Hard hat

Ears

Tool box

Feet

Body

2 Draw in her face, ears and hair.

Draw in the details on the clothes and boots.

Add tools to her tool belt.

3 colour her in!

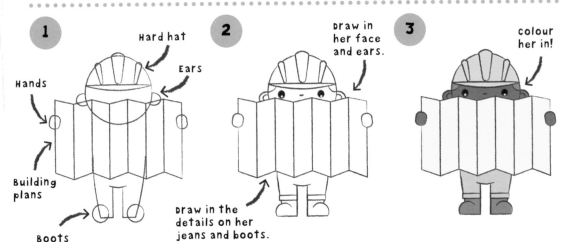

1

Hard hat

Ears

Hands

Building plans

Boots

2 Draw in her face and ears.

Draw in the details on her jeans and boots.

3 colour her in!

Erase all unwanted construction lines.

You could add these kawaii builders to a construction scene.

16

Draw your
own builder.

Kawaii firefighter

1

Helmet

Ears

Hose

Jacket

Fire extinguisher

Feet

2 Finish off his helmet.

Draw in his face, ears and hair.

Draw in the water.

3 colour him in!

Draw in his boots. Add details to his uniform.

1

Helmet

Ears

Jacket

Feet

Draw in his boots. Add details to his uniform.

2 Finish off his helmet.

Draw in his face, ears and hair.

3 colour him in!

Erase all unwanted construction lines.

Why not draw your kawaii firefighters helping to put out a blazing inferno?

18

Draw your own
firefighter.

Kawaii gladiator

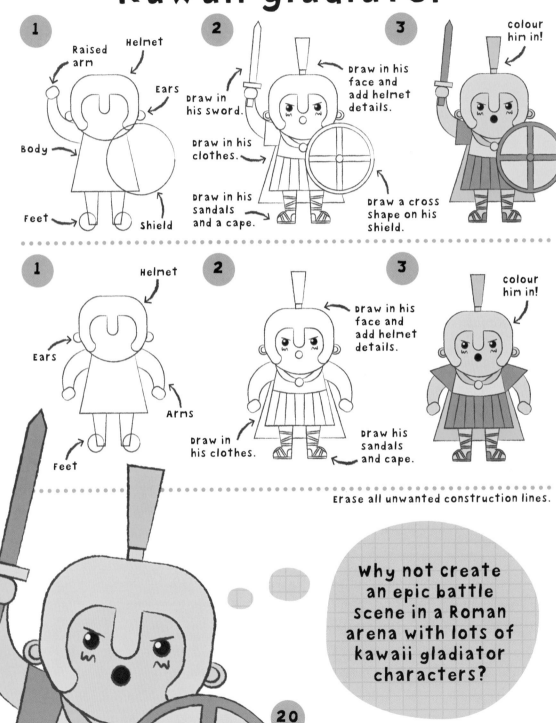

1 Raised arm · Helmet · Ears · Body · Feet · Shield

2 Draw in his sword. · Draw in his clothes. · Draw in his sandals and a cape. · Draw in his face and add helmet details.

3 colour him in! · Draw a cross shape on his shield.

1 Helmet · Ears · Arms · Feet

2 Draw in his clothes. · Draw in his face and add helmet details. · Draw his sandals and cape.

3 colour him in!

Erase all unwanted construction lines.

Why not create an epic battle scene in a Roman arena with lots of kawaii gladiator characters?

Draw your own
gladiator.

Kawaii athlete

1

Headband

Ears

Trophy

Shorts

Feet

2

Add details to trophy.

Draw in his trainers and socks.

3

Draw in his face, ears and hair.

Add details to vest and clothes.

colour him in!

1

Headband

Ears

Arms

Shorts

Feet

2

Add all details to his outfit.

5731

Draw in trainers and socks.

3

Draw in his face, ears and hair.

5731

Draw in the speed lines.

colour him in!

Erase all unwanted construction lines.

1st

Your kawaii athletes could be competing in an Olympic race!

1st

22

Draw your
own athlete.

F I N I S H

Kawaii Viking

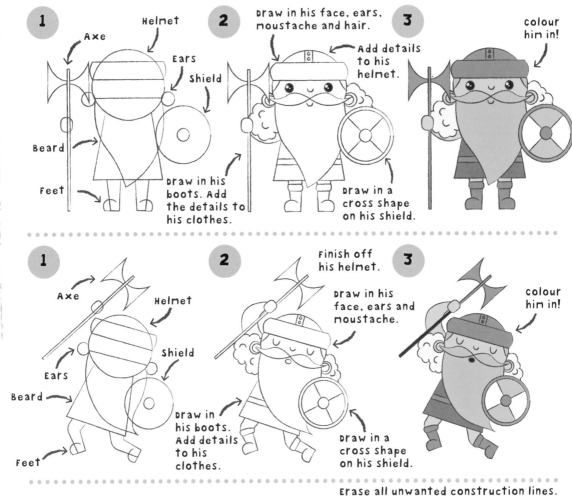

1
Axe
Helmet
Ears
Shield
Beard
Feet

Draw in his boots. Add the details to his clothes.

2 Draw in his face, ears, moustache and hair.

Add details to his helmet.

Draw in a cross shape on his shield.

3 colour him in!

1
Axe
Helmet
Ears
Shield
Beard
Feet

Draw in his boots. Add details to his clothes.

2 Finish off his helmet.

Draw in his face, ears and moustache.

Draw in a cross shape on his shield.

3 colour him in!

Erase all unwanted construction lines.

Your kawaii viking could be fighting in a battle or sailing in a viking longboat. You choose...

24

Draw your
own Viking.

25

Kawaii astronaut

1
Helmet
Arms
Finish off her space helmet.
Body

2
Draw in her face and hair.
Add a flag.
Add details to the spacesuit.

3
colour her in!

1
Legs
Body
Helmet
Arms

2
Finish off all details to spacesuit.
Draw in her face and hair.
Draw in a star.

3
colour her in!

Erase all unwanted construction lines.

Why not draw your kawaii astronauts exploring deep space?

26

Draw your own
astronaut.

Kawaii Superhero

1

Ears
Hair
Head
Arms
Cape
Legs

2 Draw her face, eyemask and crown.

Draw in her boots.

Draw in all details on her clothes.

3 colour her in!

1

Head
Ears
Hair
Arms
Legs
Cape

2 Draw in her face, eyemask and crown.

Add all details to her outfit.

Draw in her boots.

3 colour her in!

Erase all unwanted construction lines.

Why not draw your kawaii superhero battling a kawaii supervillain or rescuing someone?

28

Draw your own
superhero.

29

Kawaii chef

1
Head
Hat
Pizza
Body
Legs

2
Draw in his face, ears and moustache.
Add the top of his hat, and his hair.
Draw in his buttons, shoes and checked trousers.
Decorate the pizza.

3
colour him in!

1
covered platter
Hat
Arms
Jacket
Legs

2
Add detail to his hat.
Add wavy lines for pizza smell.

3
Draw in his face, ears and moustache.
colour him in!
Draw in his buttons, shoes and checked trousers.

Erase all unwanted construction lines.

Why not draw your kawaii chef cooking food in a busy restaurant?

30

Draw your
own chef.

Kawaii captain

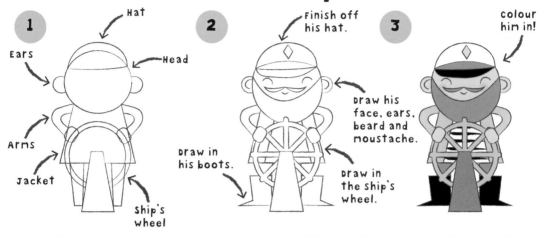

1

Hat

Ears

Head

Arms

Jacket

Ship's wheel

2

Finish off his hat.

Draw in his boots.

Draw his face, ears, beard and moustache.

Draw in the ship's wheel.

3

colour him in!

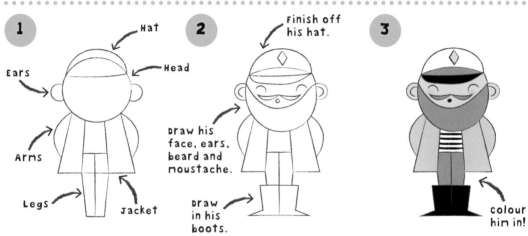

1

Hat

Ears

Head

Arms

Legs

Jacket

2

Finish off his hat.

Draw his face, ears, beard and moustache.

Draw in his boots.

3

colour him in!

Erase all unwanted construction lines.

Why not draw your kawaii sailor in his boat in stormy seas?

32

Draw your
own captain.

Kawaii artist

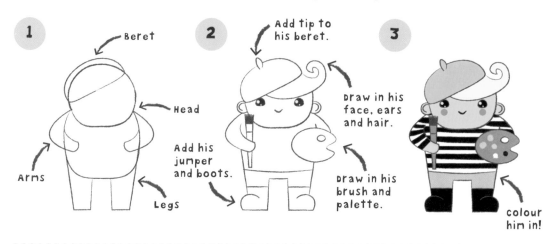

1 Beret → Head → Arms → Legs →

2 Add tip to his beret. → Draw in his face, ears and hair. → Add his jumper and boots. → Draw in his brush and palette. →

3 colour him in!

1 Head → Easel → Body → Legs → Draw in his face, ears, hair and beret. →

2 Add his boots, jumper and palette. →

3 colour him in!

Erase all unwanted construction lines.

Why not draw your kawaii artist painting a beautiful landscape?

Draw your
own artist.

Kawaii ninja

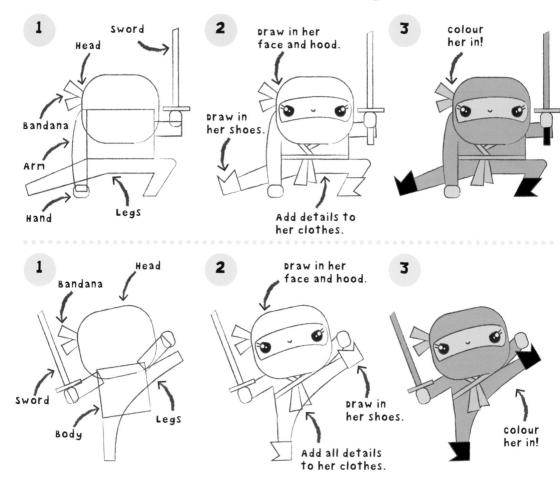

1

Sword
Head
Bandana
Arm
Hand
Legs

2

Draw in her face and hood.

Draw in her shoes.

Add details to her clothes.

3

colour her in!

1

Head
Bandana
Sword
Body
Legs

2

Draw in her face and hood.

Draw in her shoes.

Add all details to her clothes.

3

colour her in!

Erase all unwanted construction lines.

Why not draw your kawaii ninja sneaking into a closely-guarded building or temple?

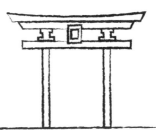

Draw your
own ninja.

Kawaii police officer

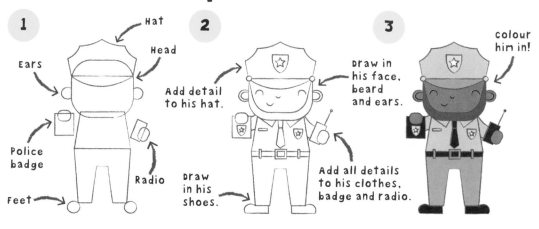

1

Ears
Police badge
Feet

Hat
Head
Radio

Add detail to his hat.
Draw in his shoes.

2

Draw in his face, beard and ears.

Add all details to his clothes, badge and radio.

3

colour him in!

1

Baton
Legs
Feet

Hat

Add detail to his hat.
Add all details to his clothes.
Hand
Draw in the shoes.

2

Draw in his face, beard and ears.

3

colour him in!

Erase all unwanted construction lines.

Why not draw your kawaii police officer chasing a kawaii criminal as he flees the scene?

Draw your own
police officer.

Kawaii doctor

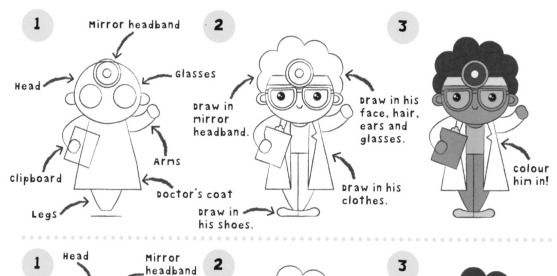

1 Mirror headband — Head — Glasses — Arms — Clipboard — Doctor's coat — Legs

2 Draw in mirror headband. Draw in his shoes.

3 Draw in his face, hair, ears and glasses. Draw in his clothes. colour him in!

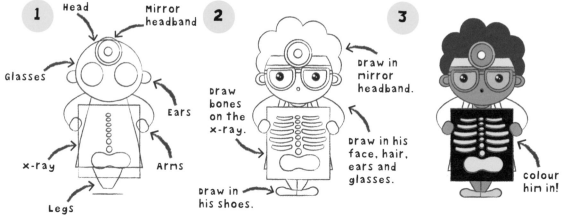

1 Head — Mirror headband — Glasses — Ears — x-ray — Arms — Legs

2 Draw bones on the x-ray. Draw in his shoes.

3 Draw in mirror headband. Draw in his face, hair, ears and glasses. colour him in!

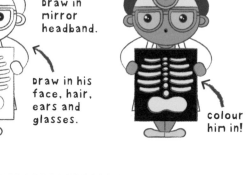

Erase all unwanted construction lines.

Why not draw your kawaii doctor attending to patients in a hospital scene, or performing an operation?

Draw your
own doctor.

Kawaii fox girl

1 Ears · Fox ears · Head · Tail · Arms · Feet

2 Draw in her eyes, mouth and hair.

Draw in all the detail for her fox costume.

3 colour her in!

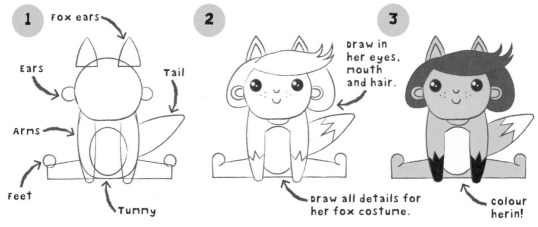

1 Fox ears · Ears · Tail · Arms · Feet · Tummy

2 Draw in her eyes, mouth and hair.

Draw all details for her fox costume.

3 colour her in!

Erase all unwanted construction lines.

You could draw your kawaii fox girl in a magical landscape with other part-human characters!

Draw your
own fox girl.

Kawaii caveman

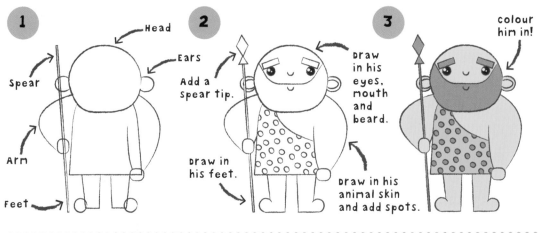

1
Head
Ears
Spear
Arm
Feet

2
Add a Spear tip.
Draw in his feet.

3
Draw in his eyes, mouth and beard.
Draw in his animal skin and add spots.
colour him in!

1
Head
Ears
Stick
Lunch
Rock

2
Add detail and wavy cooking lines to his lunch.
Draw in his eyes, mouth and beard.
Draw in the fire.

3
Add spots to his animal skin outfit.
colour him in!

Erase all unwanted construction lines.

Why not draw your kawaii caveman in his prehistoric cave or out hunting?

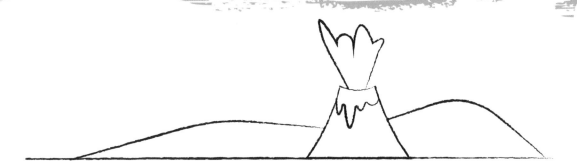

Draw your
own caveman.

Kawaii diver

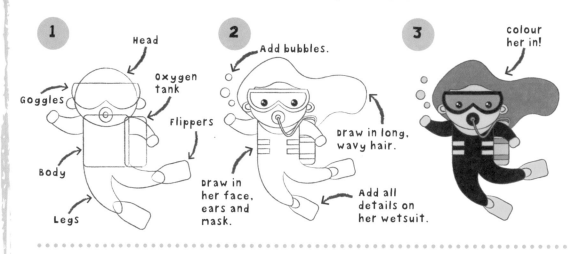

1

Head

Oxygen tank

Goggles

Flippers

Body

Legs

2

Add bubbles.

Draw in long, wavy hair.

Draw in her face, ears and mask.

Add all details on her wetsuit.

3

colour her in!

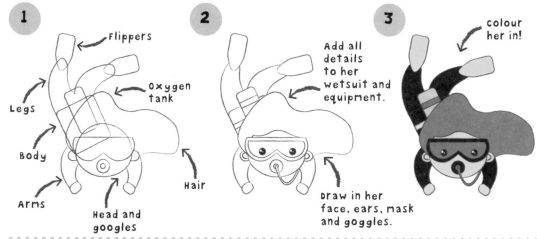

1

Flippers

Oxygen tank

Legs

Body

Hair

Arms

Head and googles

2

Add all details to her wetsuit and equipment.

Draw in her face, ears, mask and goggles.

3

colour her in!

Erase all unwanted construction lines.

Why not draw your kawaii diver swimming amongst kawaii sea creatures?

Draw your own diver.

Kawaii pilot

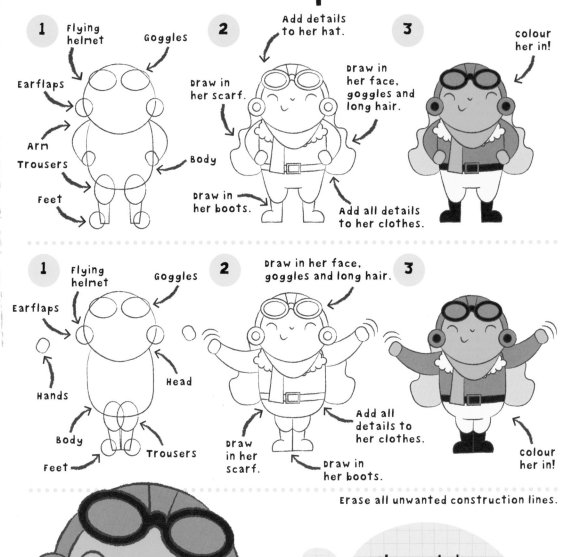

1 Flying helmet — Goggles — Earflaps — Arm — Trousers — Feet — Body

2 Add details to her hat. — Draw in her scarf. — Draw in her face, goggles and long hair. — Draw in her boots. — Add all details to her clothes.

3 colour her in!

1 Flying helmet — Goggles — Earflaps — Hands — Head — Body — Trousers — Feet

2 Draw in her face, goggles and long hair. — Draw in her scarf. — Draw in her boots. — Add all details to her clothes.

3 colour her in!

Erase all unwanted construction lines.

Why not draw your kawaii pilot flying a World War II fighter plane through the clouds?

48

Draw your own pilot.

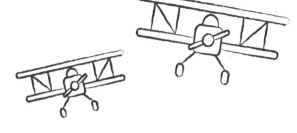

Kawaii cowboy

1

cowboy hat

Head

Arms

Legs

2

Add details to his hat.

Draw in his face, ears, moustache and hair.

Add his hands.

Draw in a rope, belt and boots.

Add in all details to his clothes.

3

colour him in!

1

Head

cowboy Hat

Body

Money bag

2

Add a scarf.

Draw in his boots.

Add a dollar sign.

Draw in his face, ears, moustache and hair.

Draw in his arms and hands.

3

colour him in!

Erase all unwanted construction lines.

Why not draw your kawaii cowboy riding on a horse through the desert?

Draw your
own cowboy.

Kawaii mermaid

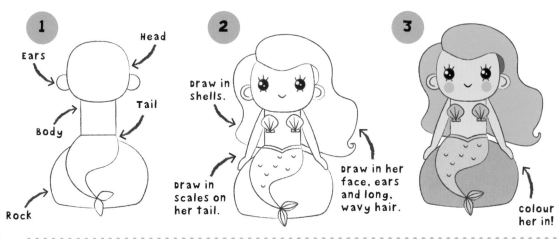

1
Ears
Head
Tail
Body
Rock

2
Draw in shells.
Draw in scales on her tail.
Draw in her face, ears and long, wavy hair.

3
colour her in!

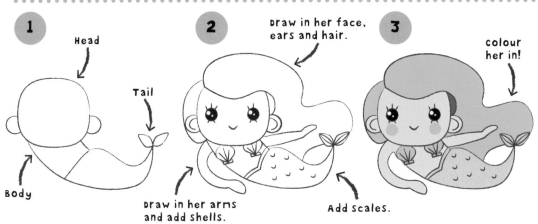

1
Head
Tail
Body

2
Draw in her face, ears and hair.
Draw in her arms and add shells.
Add Scales.

3
colour her in!

Erase all unwanted construction lines.

You could draw your kawaii mermaid underwater with lots of kawaii sea creatures!

52

Draw your
own mermaid.

Kawaii ballerina

1
Bun
Ears
Arms
Ballet shoes
Tutu

2
Add a pretty bow.
Draw in her face, ears and hair.
Add all details to her tutu and leotard.
Add ribbons.

3
colour her in!

1
Bun
Arms
Ballet shoes
Tutu

2
Add a pretty bow.
Draw in her face, ears and hair.
Add details to her tutu and leotard.
Add ribbons.

3
colour her in!

Erase all unwanted construction lines.

Why not draw your kawaii ballerina in a theatre, performing with other dancers?

54

Draw your
own ballerina.

Kawaii pharaoh

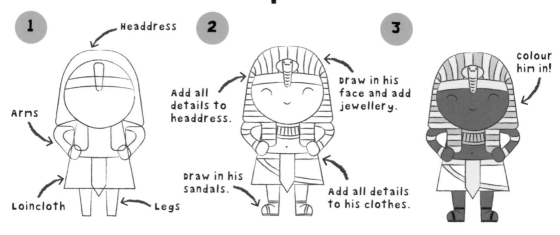

1

Headdress

Arms

Loincloth

Legs

2

Add all details to headdress.

Draw in his face and add jewellery.

Draw in his sandals.

Add all details to his clothes.

3

colour him in!

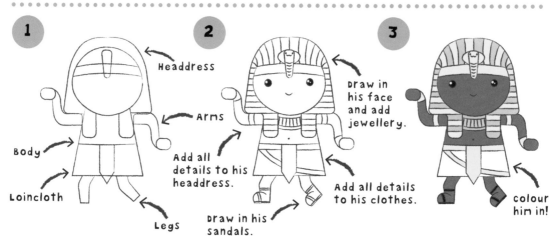

1

Headdress

Body

Loincloth

Legs

2

Arms

Add all details to his headdress.

Draw in his face and add jewellery.

Draw in his sandals.

Add all details to his clothes.

3

colour him in!

Erase all unwanted construction lines.

Why not draw your kawaii pharaoh in his palace, or watching the pyramids being built?

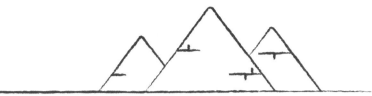

Draw your
own pharaoh.

Kawaii scientist

1 Ears / Head / Hair / Ears / Glass flask / Lab coat / Legs

2 Finish drawing her glasses. / Draw in the flask with lines for fumes. / Draw in her face, ears and hair. / Add all details to her clothes and shoes.

3 colour her in!

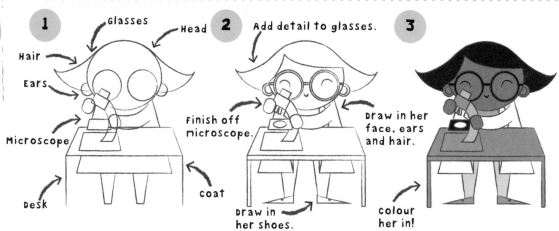

1 Glasses / Head / Hair / Ears / Microscope / Desk

2 Add detail to glasses. / Finish off microscope. / Draw in her shoes. / Draw in her face, ears and hair. / coat

3 colour her in!

Erase all unwanted construction lines.

Why not draw lots of kawaii scientists experimenting in a laboratory?

Draw your
own scientist.

Kawaii wizard

1

Hat

Ears

Wizard's robe

2

Add stars.

Add a wand.

Draw in his face, ears, hair, glasses and beard.

Draw in his hands and feet.

Finish off his robe.

3

colour him in!

1

Hat

Robes

Broomstick

Legs

Arms

2

Draw in his face, ears, hair, glasses and beard.

Add stars.

Draw in the details.

Add all details to his robes and broomstick.

Ears

3

colour him in!

Erase all unwanted construction lines.

Why not draw your kawaii wizard performing a magical spell or mixing up a smelly potion?

Draw your
own wizard. ↘

Kawaii explorer

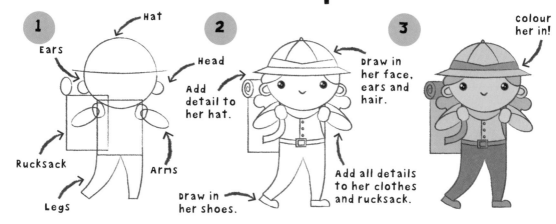

1
Hat
Ears
Head
Add detail to her hat.
Rucksack
Arms
Legs
Draw in her shoes.

2
Draw in her face, ears and hair.
Add all details to her clothes and rucksack.

3
colour her in!

1
Head
Hat
Binoculars
Arms
Body
Legs
Feet

2
Add detail to her hat.
Add all details to her clothes.
Draw in her shoes.
Draw in her face, hair and binoculars.

3
colour her in!

Erase all unwanted construction lines.

You could draw your adventurous kawaii explorer in a steamy jungle.

Draw your
own explorer.

Glossary

Gladiator someone who fought other people to the death in an arena in ancient Rome, for the entertainment of the public.

Ninja a person trained in Japanese martial arts, employed to spy on enemies or to assassinate people.

Palette a thin board on which an artist places and mixes their paint colours before using them.

Pharaoh the name for the ruler of ancient Egypt.

Viking seafaring pirates and traders from Scandinavian countries during the 8th–11th centuries AD.

Wizard a person who can perform magical spells.

Index